God

of

Islam

by
Sayed S. Akhtar Rizvi

Published by:
Tahrike Tarsile Qur'an, Inc.
Distributors of Holy Qur'an
P.O. Box 731115
Elmhurst, New York 11373-1115

First U.S. Edition 1994

Library of Congress Catalog Number Pending
British Library Cataloguing in Publishing Data

ISBN: 1-879402-27-0

Distributor in Australia:
Al-Zahra Muslim Association
1-3 Wollongong Road
Arncliffe, NSW, Australia

Distributor in England:
Murtaza Bandali / ALIF International
37 Princess Avenue
Watford, Herts WD1 7RR
England, U.K.

Distributor in Kenya:
Bilal Muslim Mission of Kenya
P.O. Box 82508
Mombasa, Kenya

Distributor in Tanzania:
World Islamic Propagation and
Humanitarian Services
P.O. Box 1895
Dar-es-Salaam, Tanzania

CONTENTS

PART ONE

PART TWO

PART THREE

1. BELIEF IN GOD: A Natural Instinct

Belief in God is as much natural as any natural instinct can be. An atheist asked Imam Jaffer Sadiq how could he convince him about the existence of God. Coming to know that the man had gone several times on a voyage, the Imam asked him. "Were you ever caught in a fierce storm in the middle of nowhere, your rudder gone, your sails torn away, and you trying desperately to keep your boat afloat?" The man said, "Yes." The Imam asked. "And sometimes perhaps even that leaking boat went down, leaving you exhausted and helpless at the mercy of the raging waves?" The answer was again "Yes."

Then the Imam asked. "Was not there, in all that black despair, a glimmer of hope in your heart that some unnamed and unknown power could still save your life?" The man agreed that there was such a power. The Imam said. "That Power is God!"

The atheist was an intelligent man. He knew the truth when he saw it.

2. TO BE OR NOT TO BE

We think about thousands and thousands of things. We imagine a horse, a man, an aeroplane, the earth, a train and a book. We see the pictures of these things displayed on the screen of our imagination.

This is called the existence in imagination (in Arabic (*wujūd-i dhihni* – وجود ذهنى).

And also a horse, a man, an aeroplane, the earth, a train or a book has its own existence outside our imagination. That is called existence outside imagination. This is the real existence (in Arabic *wujūd-i khāriji* – وجود خارجى).

Sometimes, we imagine such ideas which can never be found outside our imagination. We may imagine '2+2 = 5.' But can 2+2 be 5 in real existence? No. We may imagine that a thing exists and also does not exist at the same place at the same time. But can this happen in the world of reality? Certainly not.

Such imagined ideas which can never exist in reality are called 'Impossible' (*mumtani'u'l-wujūd* – ممتنع الوجود).

Also, we imagine a man walking at a certain time. Can this happen in reality? Remove all other ideas from your mind. Just

1

look at the imagined picture of that man walking at a particular time. Now say, is it necessary that that man should be walking at that time? Or, on the other side, is it impossible of him to be walking at that time? The answer to both questions is 'No.' Why? Because it is neither essential nor impossible for any man to walk at a given time. He may be walking; he may not be walking. So far as the reason and logic are concerned both his walking and not walking are possible - possible, but not necessary.

Such imagined ideas which have equal relation with existence and non-existence, are called 'Possible' (in Arabic *mumkinu'l-wujūd* — ممكن الوجود). They may exist in reality; they may not exist. There is nothing in their nature to demand this or that. 'To be' and 'Not to be' both are equal to such things, so far as their nature is concerned.

So far we have seen two categories of relationship between an imagined idea and its existence in reality.

(1) Where that idea has equal relation with existence and non-existence. It may exist; it may not exist. There is nothing in its nature to prefer either side.

(2) Where that idea can have absolutely no relation with existence. It, by its very nature, is non-existent.

It will appear from the above explanation that there should be a third category which would be opposite of 'Impossible' (in Arabic mumtana' al-wujud) mentioned in (2) above. This third category is of the idea which can have absolutely no relation with non-existence. By its very difinition, it is self-existent. Such an idea is called 'Essential Existence' or 'Absolute Existence' (in Arabic *wājibu'l- wujūd* – واجب الوجود)

Now the picture is complete.

3. BEGINNING POINT OF THE WORLD

There is much conflict between the points of views of atheists and those who believe in a Supreme Being Who created the world. Still, there is one important point where both are in complete agreement.

Both agree that the basic source or cause of the universe is Eternal - it has no beginning and no end; it was always and will remain for ever. In other words, it is self-existent or 'Wajib-ul-wujud.'

The reason for this idea is very simple: as every thing in this universe falls under the category of 'possible' (in Arabic mumkin al-wujud), it has equal relation with existence and non-existence. Once these things did not exist; now they exist; sometime in future, they will cease to exist. By their nature, they cannot demand to exist or to cease to exist. Therefore, there MUST be a source or cause to bring them into existence or to terminate their existence.

And (it is the important point) that source or cause should not itself be just a 'Possible' (mumkin al-wujud), otherwise it will itself need a source or cause to bring it into existence. And this chain of cause and effect MUST stop on a cause which needs no outside source or cause for its existence. It means that the final source or cause of bringing this universe into existence MUST be 'self-existent.'

As I explained above, even the atheists accept this point, because they say that nothing can come out of nothing, and, therefore, the basic source of existence must be eternal. It is from ever and will remain for ever.

Now comes the first difference. The atheists say that that eternal source of existence is 'Matter.' The believers say that that eternal source of existence is God.

We will discuss it afterwards. Here it is enough to establish a common ground of belief, and that is the faith that the basic source or cause of the existence of the universe is Eternal - without beginning and without end.

4. ESSENTIAL QUALITIES OF THE ETERNAL

A. By its very difinition, Eternal is Self-existent. It could never have been non-existent nor can it ever be terminated. In other words, it has no beginning - because if we suppose for it a beginning we must admit that it was non-existent before that beginning. But we already know that it could never have been non-existent.

Therefore, we must accept that the Eternal has no beginning - it is ever-existent.

3

B. By the same reason, it can have no end. It is everlasting, because it can never be non-existent.

C. The Eternal must be self-sufficient. In other words, it should be above all needs; it should not be in need of anything. Because, if it needs anything, it will be dependent upon that thing. But by its very definition, the Eternal does not depend upon anything, as it is Self-existent. In other words, the Eternal must have absolute perfection.

D. The Eternal can be neither compound nor mixture.

A compound or mixture depends for its existence upon its parts or components. As we accept that Eternal is Self-existent, we cannot admit that its existence depends upon its components or parts.

Moreover, look at any mixture or compound. You will find that the components or parts existed BEFORE the resulting mixture or compound. As the Eternal has no beginning, we cannot say that anything preceded it in existence. Otherwise, we will have to imagine a beginning point for the Eternal which is admittedly wrong.

E. The Eternal can be neither a body nor a surface neither a line nor a point.

A body, by its nature, needs space to be in. As we have already seen, the Eternal should not be in need of anything. It follows that the Eternal cannot be a body.

In real existence, a surface needs a body; a line needs a surface; a point needs a line. Eternal needs nothing. Therefore, the Eternal is neither a surface, line nor a point. Nor can it be anything which is found in a body, like dimension, color, smell, position, condition or other such things which are called incorporeal (in Arabic *'araḍ* – عرض) in philosophical language, because such things depend on a substance or body for their existence - they are not self-existent.

F. The Eternal should not be subject to any change, because if that change be for the better, it would mean that the Eternal before that change was not perfect, i.e., it was in need of something. But we have already said that the Eternal cannot need anything.

And if that change be for the worse, it would mean that the Eternal is now in need of something to make it perfect. And, as just explained, it is not possible.

And if that change is just to the same level of perfection, then what is the need or use of such a change?

In fact, the changes may occur either in a substance (body, matter) or in its incorporeal qualities like color, dimension etc. But it has just been proved that the Eternal can be neither a substance nor an incorporeal quality of another substance.

G. The Eternal must be a living being. Because it is agreed that the Eternal is the source and cause of the existence of the Universe. And also it is agreed that nothing can come out of nothing. Now, as we find abundance of life in the Universe, we have to admit that the source of all these living things must itself be All-life. It could not bestow life if it had itself no life.

H. The Eternal source of world must be all-knowing (Omniscient). The intricate design of a single atom shows the perfect wisdom embodied in it. The elaborate system and perfect design of universe leaves no doubt that whoever or whatever is the source or cause of the universe is all-knowing.

I. By the same reasoning the Eternal source or cause of the universe MUST be All-powerful (Omnipotent).

5. IS MATTER ETERNAL?

The atheists maintain that the matter is the Eternal source of the universe. It needs no great intelligence to see that matter does not possess any of the qualities of the Eternal mentioned in the previous chapter.

Matter has body and as such it needs space. It is divisible and as such it is made up of several parts. It is constantly changing.

But the atheists maintain that matter has no beginning and no end; and, therefore, it is eternal.

But the recent theories challenge these two last assumptions of atheism.

6. MATTER BEGINS AND ENDS

What is 'matter'? It is "substance of which a physical thing is made." Or "anything which has the property of occupying space and the attributes of gravity and inertia."

Before going further, it is necessary to point out one important thing. There are, in every branch of science, certain ideas which have no existence in reality. Yet they are assumed to exist in reality just to make it easy for the beginners to understand the arguments of that subject.

Take for example Geometry. They teach the children that 'point' is a thing having neither length, breadth nor depth. Such a thing has no physical existence. They teach that 'line' is a thing having only length, but neither breadth or depth. This also has no physical existence. In fact, it is only by taking a body (which has all three dimensions - length, breadth and depth) and sub-dividing it in imagination that we can understand the conception of surface, line and point.

Still students of geometry are taught as though these things have real physical existence. It is done not to deceive the student, but to make it easier for him to understand geometry.

Likewise, in chemistry, the student is taught that matter can neither be created nor destroyed. But it is just a stepping stone so that students can understand further arguments.

Also, it is for this reason that students of chemistry are taught separate conservation of matter and energy.

But, in classical mechanics, mass and energy are considered to be conserved separately; in atomic and nuclear reactions, matter can be converted into energy and vice verse ... so far as chemistry is concerned, the law of conservation of matter, i.e., matter can neither be created nor destroyed, can be assumed to be true."

So you see, the theory that matter is eternal (it is neither created nor destroyed) is just an assumption for the purpose of simplifying the subject for chemistry students.

It is a fact that matter changes into energy. So it is not a thing everlasting nor is it a thing which does not change. Thus, we see that matter does not pass the test of eternity - it is not without end, and it is not without change. And as it is supposed that energy can be changed into matter, it is admitted that matter has a beginning. So, it is not eternal - it is not without beginning.

It is assumed that when the matter changes into energy, it remains in that form, and, thus they try to prove that matter is everlasting. But what is Energy? It is the "capacity of matter to perform work as the result of its motion or its position in relation to forces acting upon it." So, the energy is not a thing having independent existence. It is an incorporeal thing, i.e., it depends upon a matter or substance for its existence. By its very definition, it cannot be found except in a matter. As energy is a dependent thing, it cannot be an eternal thing.

7. TWO SUPPOSITIONS

Now, it should be mentioned here that there are two hypotheses, i.e., tentative theories, in science about the creation or beginning of the universe (Universe: all created or existing things). First, there is the evolutionary theory. This theory says that all the material in the universe was formerly concentrated in a sort of 'primeval' (i.e. ancient) nebula or cloud; that the universe was created at one particular moment and that it will eventually die.

If this idea is correct then that primeval cloud cannot be said to be eternal. A thing which dies, which comes to an end, cannot be said, by any stretch of imagination, to be selfexistent or everlasting or eternal.

The second hypothesis is called "Steady state" theory. It maintains that the universe has always existed and will exist for ever, and that fresh matter is continually being created. Now the universe is a collection of matter; and they believe that matter is continually being created. In other words, the universe is a compound of created things. How can a collection of created things be called "Eternal" (without beginning) is beyond credulity.

Thus it is clear that, whatever view one takes, matter cannot be proved to be eternal (without beginning and without end).

Now, that matter is believed to be constantly created afresh; it is known to change into energy; it is known to need a shape and a place; it is subject to division and constant changes, can it be said that matter is eternal when all its qualities are those of Transient (mumkin al-wujud)?

Five atheists had had a discussion with the Holy Prophet, at the end of which he told them:

"This universe is of such a nature that some of its parts are dependent on some other parts; they cannot exist without those other parts, just as some parts of a structure depend upon other parts for their strength and existence. And the whole universe is, in this respect, like that building." Now, tell me, if that part (which is dependent upon other part for its strength and existence) is eternal inspite of its dependence and need, then what would have been its quality had it been just transient (possible, not eternal)?

Yes. Let the atheists say what it would have been like if the matter were not eternal.

8. MATTER NOT THE SOURCE OF LIFE

Now, we come to the last three qualities mentioned in the previous chapter. We have already accepted the 'atheists' notion that nothing comes out of nothing. Now, we see in the universe a most intelligent design and pattern and a most perfect coordination in this unparalleled system. And we see it teeming with life. And, admittedly, matter has no life, and hence no power or knowledge.

If matter was the cause or source of the universe, the universe would have been without life; it would have been without system and coordination, because it could not give to universe what it did not possess itself. Is there any need to emphasize in so many words that matter cannot be considered as the source of universe.

9. THEISM VERSUS ATHEISM

Here I give the translation of the discussion of the Holy Prophet with the atheists, a part of which has been copied earlier:

The Holy Prophet asked them: "What is the reason of your belief that the universe has neither beginning nor end and that these things are from ever and will remain for ever?

Atheists: We believe only what we see. As we have not seen the beginning of the universe, therefore we say that it has always existed, and as we have not seen its extinction, we say that it will remain for ever.

Holy Prophet: Well, have you seen that the universe is without beginning and without end?

Atheists: No, we have not seen its being without beginning nor have we seen its being without end.

Holy Prophet: Then how do you believe in its eternity? And why should your view be preferred to the view of that person who believes the universe to be transient because he has not seen its being without beginning or without end?

Then after some more arguments the Holy Prophet asked: "Can you tell me whether the days (time) which have passed on this earth were finite (limited) or infinite (limitless)? If you say that the time which has passed so far was limitless, then how the later time came in if the former did not pass away?

"And if you say that the time is finite (limited) then you will have to admit that it is not eternal."

Atheists: Yes, it is finite.

Holy Prophet: Well, you were saying that universe is eternal, nor created nor finite. Do you realize what is the implication of your admission that time is finite? What were you denying? What have you admitted?

The atheists accepted that their belief was not correct.

Incidentally, this argument of the Holy Prophet shows that 'time' has unbreakable relation with matter. Otherwise, he could not have introduced the element of time in the discussion about matter. The beauty of this can best be appreciated by only those who have studied the theory of Relativity.

10. SOME TALKS

The most simple arguments of the ancients on this topic are still valid, inspite of all the complexity of the modern science.

An old woman was spinning yarn. Someone asked her why did she believe in God. She stopped her hand and the spindle stopped. She said: "You see, a simple spindle needs a hand to make it revolve. Can you think that this sun, this moon, these stars, all this world moves without any guiding hand?"

Hadhret Ali ibn Abi Talib (a.s.) was asked for a proof of the existence of the Almighty Designer. He replied, the traces of the camel lead one to conclude that a camel has passed that way. The traces of human feet indicate a man's trek. Do not this magnificent universe, with all its sublimity and this lowly point (the earth) with all its solidity point to the existence of the Almighty Allah, the Sublime and the Omniscient?

Once Abu Shakir Disani, an atheist, came to Imam Jafar Sadiq (a.s.) and asked him to guide him to the recognition of "my Supreme Lord." Imam (a.s.) asked him to take a seat. There arrived a child playing with an egg in his hand. Imam (a.s.) taking the egg from him, addressed Abu Shakir Disani saying,

9

"Here is a mysterious fortress enclosed within a hard shell, underneath which is a fine wrapping covering molten silver (the albumen of the egg) and some molden gold (the yellow yolk). The molten gold does not get alloyed with the molten silver, nor does the molten silver get alloyed with the molten gold. (Yet both are semi-fluid and they should have mixed together on jerking). They retain their separate states. No artist comes out of it to say that he has made therein any amendment nor does any vitiating agent enter it to tell of any vitiation therein.

"Nor is it known whether it is designed to produce a male or a female. Pea-birds of florid coloration issue therefrom. Do you think it has a Designer (the Omniscient Creator)? Who has painted all this inside it? And how about the chick? Who designed all these variegated hues, the feathers, the limbs, the paintings, the feet, the beak, the wings, the eyes, the ears, the nose, the crop, the joints etc. seeing that no one entered it?"

Abu Shakir, according to the narration, was absorbed in his thoughts for sometime with his head bowed low, and then he suddenly declared, "I bear witness that there is no god but Allah, the One without peer and I bear witness that Muhammed (S) is His slave and Prophet, and that you are the Imam and Proof from Allah, toward His creation and I turn away from my erstwhile attitude."

11. RELIGION VERSUS DARWINISM

When Darwin first published his treatise 'The Origin of Species' in 1859, he stirred a tumultous opposition from the religious groups. This religious opposition was based, mainly, upon two factors:

1.Darwin asserted - with convincing proofs - that the universe was not made in six days, as described in the Bible, but in a very very long time with so many states between the first state and the present form; and

2.he denied - without any valid reason, of course - the need of a Supreme Being (God) in the scheme of the universe.

The Jews and the Christians of that time believed in the six-day-creation quite literally. They could not be expected to swallow the idea of the protracted creation easily. And so the conflict between Christianity and Science reached it climax in the latter half of the 19th century.

But what about the Muslims?

The Quran says that the skies and the earth (mark it! Not the whole universe. Not the Man. Only the skies, earth and the vegetation) were created in six 'ayyam.' The word 'ayyam' has two meanings: 'days' and 'periods.' The Sunni commentators of Quran generally followed Kaabul-Ahbar, a former Jew converted to Islam in the days of the second khalifa. It was natural for him to explain those verses of Quran in the light of his previous learning. So, he imported every Jewish legend into Islam.

Though the Quran was silent about the details, the Muslims interpreted the 'Ayats' in such a way that every detail of Genesis (of the Bible) was incorporated in the commentaries of Quran and thus became a part of Sunni religious belief.

But the Shia commentators rejected the idea of six-days-creation right from the early days of Islam. According to them, 'ayyam' in those verses meant 'Periods,' and not the 'days.' For instance, see the commentaries of Quran by Ali ibn Ibrahim Qummi (died sometime after A.D. 919) and Muhsin Faiz (died in A.D. 1680). Also, see the Dictionary of Quran and Traditions, by Shaikh Fakhruddin Tahiri (died A.D. 1676). According to them the Quran says that the skies and the earth were created in six periods. (Or should we say 'in six stages'!)

Therefore, we, the Shia Muslims, have nothing against the theory of the gradual process of Creation, which is embodied in the theory of Evolution. More than that, ours is not a belated attempt at re-interpreting our religion - as Christians are doing now to cover the Christianity's defeat by Science. We were thinking on the same lines one thousand years before Darwin.

But it must be mentioned here that the acceptance of gradual creation does not mean that we endorse the hypothesis of the Evolution. The Evolutionists claim that "(1) living things change from generation to generation producing descendants with new characteristics; (2) this process has produced all the groups and kind of things now living as well as others now extinct; (3) all these different living things are related to each other."

But, as I have mentioned in *Need of Religion* there is not a single fossil-evidence to show that a member of lower species developed into a higher species. It is for this reason that Dr. T.N. Tahmisian, a physiologist for the Atomic Energy Commission, said: "Scientists who go about teaching that evolution is a fact of life, are great con men, and the story they are telling may be the greatest hoax ever. In explaining evolution we do not have one iota of fact."

It is one thing to say, as we say (and the fossils and scientific data support us) that God created this universe in stages and created the things and living beings on earth one after another with time gaps in between; and quite another, as the Darwinists or neo-Darwinists say (and have no evidence to prove it) that the living things on this earth developed from non-living matter and that a monocell like plankton developed stage by stage to become a human being.

12. WHERE THE DARWINISTS WENT ASTRAY

So much about the first ground of the conlict between religion and science. Now we come to the second ground of conflict, i.e., the denial of God. Here we, the Shia Muslims, as well as other religions (and many scientists of the present generation) are totally against the Darwinism.

Let me explain our view in a few sentences.

The whole deliberation on Evolution attempts to answer the question, "How the universe came into being?" But it does not touch the other big question: "By whom was it created?" But Darwin and his followers said that as they could explain the sequence of the creation and its working method, so it was automatically proved that there was no God. It is just like saying, "as I can explain the working of an automobile and can guess the sequence of its manufacturing, so it is automatically proved that there is no manufacturer of that car."

It may seem absurd as I have put it on paper here. But the more you read their denials of God, the more you will be remined of this fallacy in their arguments.

Now let us look at one more fallacy of atheism. I have already dealt with this fallacy in previous chapters. But here it is repeated to complete the picture. They assert that 'thing' cannot come of 'Nothing.' Therefore, according to them, it was wrong to say that God created the universe out of nothing. There must be a source of every thing. So, they believe that the Matter is eternal; and every thing is a development of the eternal Matter.

This line of argument goes straight until it reaches the stage where begins the phenomenon called "Life." Nobody has ever succeeded in solving the mysteries of Life. Nobody knows where Life came from. Having rejected the belief in God, the atheists are compelled to say, "We do not know; but Life must have come from the Matter." Now, Matter is lifeless. If 'thing' cannot come from 'Nothing,' how can the 'Life' come from 'Lifeless?"

Not only this. Let us proceed further. As they say, there must be a source of everything. And as every body knows, the Matter is a 'Thing.' What was the source of 'Matter'?

These phenomena of the universe cannot be explained without stopping at a certain point and believing that the universe began from it. The atheists say that the Matter is that beginning point. But the Matter is Lifeless. So, the existence of life cannot be explained by this theory. And the Matter is Senseless. The existence of Sense and Wisdom in the animals and human beings cannot be explained by it.

Therefore, if we are to have a satisfactory theory for the existence of the universe as a whole, we have to accept that there IS an Eternal Being Who is the Source of Existence, the Source of Life and the Source of Wisdom. That Being is God.

13. RUSSELL'S ARGUMENTS

Why I am not a Christian is a collection of Bertrand Russell's essays and papers "on religion and related subjects." Professor Paul Edwards, the editor of the book, says that these essays are "perhaps the most moving and the most graceful presentation of the free-thinker's position since the days of Hume and Voltaire."

This statement, coupled with the name of Russell, was enough to compel one to study the book with high expectation of scholarly and logical discourses on the subject of religion. Whether those expectations were justified will be seen from a few comments appended below:-

The first thing which comes before the eyes is the inconsistency of the arguments. Russell called himself a free-thinker, and during a debate with Rev. F.C.Copleston he said that he was not an atheist but an agnostic.

The position of atheists is that non-existence of God can be proved. The agnostics, on the other hand, say that "man does not and cannot in the nature of things know anything about a spiritual existence, either of God or man or of any after-death state." They assert that "man's only cognition can be of the phenomenal world (that is, the world which may be perceived by one of the five senses)". According to them, it does not mean that there may not be a nominal entity (that is, an entity known through intellectual institution only) or soul behind the phenomenal world.

The agnostics repudiate even atheism or materialism on the ground that these theories are dogmatic. They say that if you cannot know a thing, you have no right to reject it. An agnostic's one and only answer to all questions concerning soul, God or spiritual existence is that "we do not know and there are so far no reasonable grounds for believing that we shall ever know. In other words, man, being finite, can never comprehend Infinite."

Rev. Copleston had asked Russell at the beginning of their debate (in 1948): "Perhaps you would tell me if your position is that of agnosticism or of atheism. I mean, would you say that non-existence of God can be proved?" Russell replied: "No, I should not say that; my position is agnostic."

If Russell believed in agnosticism, then his only answer about all questions concerning God, or life after death should have been "I do not know." Instead, he declared right on the jacket of the book, "I believe that when I die I shall rot, and nothing of my ego will survive."

Another example, Russell says at the beginning of the preface, "I think all the great traditions of the world - Buddhism, Hinduism, Christianity, Islam and Communism - both untrue and harmful. It is evident as a matter of logic that, since they disagree, not more than one of them can be true."

After this statement, one would expect him to look at each of the above religions in turn to prove why even one of them was not true. But he did not feel obliged in any of his essays to bring this argument to its logical end. He just said that, "since they disagree, not more than one of them can be true," and then arbitrarily concluded that not even one of them was true!

This type of inconsistency goes on from essay to essay; and one finishes the book with a feeling that if these essays would have been written by a lesser being than Russell, the publishers would not have designed to publish them.

The first article *Why I am Not A Christian* was delivered as a lecture in 1927; Russell has tried in this lecture to repudiate the arguments of Church for the existence of God.

He says:

"Perhaps the simplest and easiest to understand is the argument of the First Cause. (It is maintained that every thing we see in this world has a cause, and as you go back in the chain of causes further and further you must come to a First Cause, and to that First Cause you give the name of God.)...I may say that when I was a young man and was debating these questions very seriously in my mind, I for a long time accepted the argument of the First Cause, until one day, at the age of 18, I read John Stuart Mill's Autobiography and I there found this sentence: 'My father taught me that the question, 'Who made me?' cannot be answered since it immediately suggests the further question, 'Who made God?' That very simple sentence showed me, as I still think, the fallacy in the argument if the First Cause."

Now, Russell has, perhaps unwittingly, misquoted the arguments of believers. To refresh the memory, the reader os advised to read again Chapter 2 and 3 of this book. There he will find, *inter alia,* the following sentences:-

"As every thing in this universe falls under the category of *'mumkinu'l-wujud'* (Transient), it has equal relation with existence and non-existence. Once these things did not exist; now they exist; sometime in future they will cease to exist. By their nature, they cannot demand to exist or cease to exist. Therefore, there **must** be a source or cause to bring them to existence or to terminate their existence."

And then comes the important point which Russell had missed. The point is that source or cause should not itself be just Transient. Otherwise it will itself need a source or cause to bring it into existence. And this chain if cause and effect **must** stop on a cause which needs no outside source or cause for its existence. It means that the final source or cause of this universe **must** be 'Self-existent'.

If one compares the Islamic version of the argument of 'The First Cause' (as given in the book) with the version of the Church as presented be Russell at the beginning, one finds two important differences; He said, "Everything we see in the world has a cause." But he should have said, "Every thing we see in this world is transient and as such must have a cause for its existence."

Again, he said, "As you go back in the chain of causes further and further you must come to a First Cause." But he should have said, "You must come to a Cause which is not transient, which is Self-existent (whose very essence is the existence itself)."

Read his version with these amendments, and see how his objections loose every weight.

Russell thought it sufficient to scoff at this argument off-handedly. "I can illustrate what seems to me (the believers') fallacy. Every man who exists has a mother and it seems to me (their) argument is that therefore the human race must have a mother, but obviously the human race hasn't a mother."

It seems to me that it is Russell who is indulging in fallacy. He has failed to note that the believers do not say that 'every transient thing has a transient cause, therefore, the whole universe should have a transient cause.'

Our argument is that, all the components of the universe are transient, and as a collection of billions of transient things is still transient, the whole universe is still transient, and as such must have an external cause to bring it into existence. And that cause must be Self-existent. And as He is Self-existent, the question, 'Who made God?' doesn't arise.

14. CREATION BY CHANCE?
WITHOUT A CREATOR?

Russell further wrote, "If there can be anything without a cause it may just as well be the world as God."

The reason why the world could not have existed or come into being without a Cause, is that its components some times exist and some times cease to exist. So there is nothing in their essence, in their nature, to demand existence. If they exist, it must be because of a hand which tilted the scale in favor of existence; if they cease to exist it must be because that hand has now tipped the scale towards non existence.

Russell: "Nor there is any reason why it (the world) should not have always existed."

The claim that the world may have always existed is refuted by all prevalent theories of science: This is quite apart from the fact that a collection of transient things could not exist "always".

The reader should read Chapter 7 again, where he will find that whatever view one takes, matter cannot be proved to be eternal (without beginning and without end).

Again he says: "There is no reason why the world could not have come into being without a cause."

Before commenting further on this sentence, let me quote his words (from the same article) where he refutes the idea that there is any "natural law". He writes:-

"There is, as we all know, a law that if you throw dice you will get double sixes only once in thirty six times, and we do not regard that as evidence that the fall of the dice is regulated by design; on the contrary, if the double sixes came every time, we should think that there was a design."

Here Russell admits that if events appeared in the same sequence again and again it would be a proof that there was a design. Now, one wonders why he did not spare a few moments looking at the well-planned and superbly-executed movements of the galaxies, stars, planets and moons? Let us suppose that there is someone in outer space who has never heard about earth or human beings. Then one day he sees a space-ship streaking past and after some time another one, and then another one. Of course, their paths are not the same, and the gap between their appearances is not systematic so that it might be measured and estimated in advance. But he knows that each space-ship contains thousands of parts which are well connected to each other and together they form a superbly efficient apparatus.

What would Russell think of him if he were to declare that those space-ships had come into being without a creator?

And how strongly would he have condemned the arrogance of that inhabitant of outer space, if all the space-ships would have been well regulated in their paths and frequency?

And, remember that those space-ships have no connection with each other. Compare that with this universe of uncounted millions of galaxies, each having millions of solar systems, each containing numerous planets, and the planets having numerous moons etc.

And all of them "bound" together in the chain of gravity, each influencing its neighbor, and in turn being influenced by it. And then think that Mr. Russell says that it was not proof of any design.

Frank Allen, former professor of Biophysics in University of Manitoba, Canada, writes in his articles, *The Origin of the World: By Chance of Design,* "If in the origin of life there was no design, then living matter must have arisen by chance. Now chance, or probability as it is termed, is a highly developed mathematical theory which applies to that vast range of knowledge that are beyond absolute certainty. This theory puts us in possession of the soundest principles on which to discriminate truth from error, and to calculate the likelihood of the occurrence of and particular form of an event."

Proteins are the essential constituents of all living cells, and they consist of the five elements, carbon, hydrogen, nitrogen, oxygen and sulphur, with possibly 40,000 atoms in the ponderous molecule. As there are 92 chemical elements in Nature, all distributed at random, the chance that these five elements may come together to form the molecule, the quantity of matter of matter that must be continually shaken up, and the length of time necessary to finish this task, can all be calculated. A Swiss mathematician, Charles Eugen Guye,[1] has made the computation and finds that the odds against such an occurrence are 10^{160} to 1, or only chance in 10^{160}, that is, 10 multiplied by itself 160 times, a number far too large to expressed in words.[2] The amount of matter to be shaken together to produce a single molecule of protein would be millions of times greater than that in the whole universe. For it to occur on the earth alone would require many, almost endless billions (10^{243})of years. (For this number, write 243 zeros after one!)

Proteins are made from long chains called amino acids. The way those are put together matters enormously. If in the wrong way they will not sustain life and may be poisons. Professor J.B.Leathes (England) has calculated that the links in the chain of quite a simple protein could be put together in millions of ways (10^{48}) (that is 48 zeros written after number 1). It is impossible for all these chances to have coincided to build one molecule of protein.

---

1   Quoted by V.H. Mottran in the Organ Corporation, Liner, April 22nd 1948.

2   To write this number, you will have to add 160 zeros after one.

But there are incalculable billions on molecules of protein in only one human body, let alone the whole earth.

They are created systematically and still Russell clings to his theory of chance!

Frank Allen goes on to say, "But proteins as chemicals are without life. It is only where the mysterious life comes into them that they live. Only Infinite Mind, that is God, could have foreseen that such a molecule could be the abode of life, could have constructed it, and made it live."

Russell has endeavored to challenge this argument in these words, "You all know the argument from design: everything in the world is made just so that we can manage to live in it. That is the argument from design. It sometimes takes a rather curious form; for instance, it is argued that rabbits have white tails in order to be easy to shoot. I do not know how rabbits would view that application. It is an easy argument to parody. You all know Voltaire's remark, that obviously the nose was designed to be such as to fit spectacles. That sort of parody had turned out to be not nearly so wide of the mark as it might have seemed in the eighteenth century, because since the time of Darwin we understand much better why living creatures are adapted to their environment. It is not that their environment was made to be suitable to them, but they grew to be suitable to it, and that is the basis of adaption. There is no evidence of design about it."

Let us suppose, for the time being, that the living creatures adapted themselves to their environment. But was Russell really blind to the fact that long before the "living creatures" came on this earth, its atmosphere, its whole structure, together with its relations with sun and other planets and moon had been "made" in such a way that the life became possible at all. Does he want us to believe that the living things, that is, the animals and man, before their own existence, influenced the whole system of universe in general, and that of this earth in particular, so that they might be born here untold millions of year in future?

Frank Allen writes in the same article:

The adjustments of the earth for life are far too numerous to be accounted for by chance. First, the earth is a sphere freely poised in space in daily rotation on its polar axis, giving the alteration of day and night, and in yearly revolution around the sun. These motions give stability to its orientation in space, and, coupled with the inclination (23 degrees) of the polar axis to the place of its revolution (the ecliptic), affords regularity to the seasons, thus doubling the habitable area of the earth and providing a greater diversity of plant life than a stationary globe could sustain.

Secondly, the atmosphere of life supporting gases is sufficiently high (about 500 miles) and dense to blanket the earth against the deadly impact of twenty million meteors that daily enter it at speeds of about thirty miles per second. Among many other functions the atmosphere also maintains the temperature within safe limits for life; and carries the vital supply of fresh water vapor far inland from the oceans to irrigate the earth, without which it would become a lifeless desert. Thus the oceans, with the atmosphere, are the balance-wheel of Nature.

Four remarkable properties of water, its power of absorbing vast quantities of oxygen at low temperatures, its maximum density at 4 degrees 'C' above freezing whereby lakes and rivers remain liquid, the lesser density of ice than water so that it remains on the surface, and the power of releasing great quantities of heat as it freezes, preserve life in oceans, lakes and rivers throughout the long winters.

The dry land is a stable platform for much terrestrial life. The soil provides the minerals which plant life assimilates and transforms into needful foods for animals. The presence of metals near the surface renders the arts of civilization possible.

The diminutive size of the earth compared with the immensity of space is sometimes disparagingly referred to. If the earth were as small as the moon, if one-fourth its present diameter, the force of gravity (one sixth that of the earth) would fail to hold both atmosphere and water, and temperatures would be fatally extreme. If double its present diameter, the enlarged earth would have four times its present surface and twice its force of gravity, the atmosphere would be dangerously reduced in height, and pressure would be increased from 15 to 30 pounds per square inch with serious repercussions upon life. The winter areas would be seriously diminished. Communities of people would be isolated, travel and communication rendered difficult or almost impossible.

If our earth were of the size of the sun, but retaining its density, gravity would be 150 times as great, the atmosphere diminished to about four miles in height, evaporation of water rendered impossible, and pressure increased to over a ton per square inch. A one-pound animal would weigh 150 pounds, and human beings reduced in size to that of say, a squirrel. Intellectual life would be impossible to such creatures.

If the earth were removed to double its present distance from the sun, the heat received would be reduced to one-fourth of its present amount, the orbital velocity would be only one half, the winter season would be doubled in length and life would be frozen out. If its solar distance were halved, the heat received would be four times as great, the orbital velocity would be doubled, seasons would be halved in length, if changes could even be effected, and the planet would be too parched to sustain life. In size and distance from the sun, and in orbital velocity, the earth is able to sustain life, so that mankind can enjoy physical, intellectual and spiritual life as it now prevails.

15. THE SAFEST COURSE FOR AGNOSTICS

As was mentioned earlier, Russell claimed to be an agnostic. If we take that claim on its face-value, then the best and safest course for him would have been to believe in a Creator and Day of Judgement.

Here is a tradition of Imam Ja'far as-Sadiq (p.b.u.h.):

Ibn Abi al-Awja' and Ibn al-Muqaffa' were sitting in Masjidu'l-haram at the time of pilgrimage, with some of their fellow atheists. (They pretended to be Muslims just to save their skins; but were always openly arguing against the belief in God.) Ibn al-Muqaffa' said pointing towards the space around Ka'bah: "Do you see this mob? There is none among them who may be called human being except that old man (that is, Imam Ja'far as-Sadiq - p.b.u.h.). As for the others, they are just cattles and animals."

Ibn Abi al-Awja' asked how could he say such a thing?

Ibn al-Muqaffa' said: "Because I found with him (the virtues and knowledge) which I did not find anywhere else."

Ibn Abi al-Awja said: "Now it is necessary to test whether what you say is true."

Ibn al-Muqaffa' tried to dissuade him from it. But Ibn Abi al-Awja' went to the Imam. He came back after sometime and said: "O 'Ibn al-Muqaffa', he is not just human being. If there were in this world a spiritual thing...which becomes a body if wishes so, and turns into a spirit if wants so, then it is he."

Ibn al-Muqaffa said: "How come?"

Ibn Abi al-Awja said, "I sat near him. When all others went away, he started talking (without my asking anything) and said", "If the fact is as they believe and it is as they (that is, the pilgrims) say, then they would be saved and you would be in trouble. And if the fact is as you (atheists) say, and not as they say, then you and they both would be equal (and no harm would come to anybody)"

I said, "May Allah have mercy on you, what is it which we say and what is it which they say? My belief and their belief is but one."

Imam said, "How could your belief and their belief be the same? They say that there is to be resurrection, and reward and punishment; and they believe that there is a God.' " (And you do not believe it).

Imam meant that if there was in reality no God and no Day of Judgement, as Ibn Abi as-Awja' said, then the believers and non believers will be in the same position after death. Both will perish for ever and nobody would suffer for his belief or disbelief. On the other hand, if there is God and a Day of Judgement, as the believers say, then after death the believers would be saved and would be blessed, while the atheists and non-believers would have to suffer. Therefore, it is the dictate of wisdom to have faith and Belief in God and Day of Judgement, to save oneself from the possibility of disgrace and eternal punishment.

The reader should also see the chapter "Pascal's Bet" in *Need of Religion.*

16. UNIVERSE: WITNESS OF ONE GOD

A unique pattern of the universe is emerging with the advent of Science. There was a time when the Earth was considered to be the center of the universe; and the universe was confined within the nine skies. Our fifth Imam Hadhret Muhammed Baqir (a.s.) explained to his companions that there were innumerable worlds besides what they knew about. But, strangely, the Muslims ignored his teachings and followed the pagan philosophers like Ptolemy who thought and taught that the Earth was stationary and the heavenly bodies revolved around it.

Consequently, the gate of knowledge remained shut against them for more than one thousand years.

Then came a time when the people explored the solar system by the help of telescopes. So, they gave the sun the place of pride. Now we know that our solar system is but an insignificant family of planets at the edge of the huge galaxy which we call the Milky Way.

We see the Moon rotating around the earth, just like a happy child dancing brightly around its mother. We know that the moon is a satellite of the planet whom we have named 'Earth.' There are eight other planets, besides our earth, in the solar system; and five of them have got satellites of their own. Mars and Neptune have two moons each; Jupiter has twelve moons and satellites; Saturn has nine and Uranus has five moons. All the moons and satellites rotate around their planets. And all these planets, in turn, rotate round the sun, which may be called the Head of the Family.

Now, let us trace back our steps, before going further.

All these stars, planets and satellites are made of atoms. And the atom itself is a miniature solar system. Formerly, it was believed that atoms were immutable entities, i.e., they could not be divided. Now the atoms are known to have so many particles; the belief in their indestructibility has been shattered away. Atoms consist of a nucleus and a number of electrons. The nucleus is built from simple particles: neutrons and protons. The nucleus is located at the center of the atom and is surrounded by electrons. It should be mentioned here, to make the picture more clear, that the nucleus of an atom is a particle of very small radius, but of exceedingly great density.

In plain words, all the atomic mass (except a negligible fraction) is concentrated in the nucleus, while the size of the nucleus is less than one hundred thousandth of the size of the atom. And don't forget that more than 100,000,000 atoms can be put side by side in one centimeter. Now, as we have stated earlier, the atom is a world in itself. The protons and neutrons behave as though they were rotating around their own axis, like rotating tops. Their spin suggests the idea of an internal rotation.

Thus, we see that there is a single pattern of operation, right from the smallest sub-atomic particles to the mighty solar system.

But this is not the end of the story.

23

As we have known, the sun, together with its family, is placed on the brink of the Milky Way. "If we could view the Milky Way from a vast distance and see it as a whole, we should observe a rather flat wheel of stars with spiral arms - something like the sparks of a Catherine wheel." It consists of many million separate stars like our sun. This system of stars is physically connected by gravitational forces and moves through space as a whole. It is called a galaxy.

If we think that our solar system is a family of stars, a galaxy may be called a very big tribe consisting of millions and millions of such families.

The multitude of galaxies were unknown in the past. By about 1920, it was thought that there were at least 500,000 galaxies. Now, with the advent of the powerful talescopes, this number rose to 100,000,000, and is being increased further day by day. So far as the eyes of the cameras and telescopes can see, there are clusters and clusters of galaxies.

Human knowledge, at present, is in its infancy. Nobody knows what is beyond these galaxies. Nor we know anything about the nature of their movement. Quran says that "Allah has decorated the nearest sky with these lamps (i.e. the stars)." So we know that we have not seen the end of even the first sky, until now. And who knows what wonders are hidden beyond the first sky! "You know nothing but a little." (Quran).

So, let us confine our talks to a little we know about. We know that the particles of atoms are rotating around their axis; satellites are rotating around their planets; planets are rotating around their stars; and stars along with their dependent families, are rotating in the galaxies.

Our faith in the Unity of God is THE PUREST in the world. We have given countless proofs for our belief in the last fourteen centuries. Now, Science has opened a new path, which, also, leads to the belief in the Unity of God. I would like to put it, briefly, in these words: 'The uniform pattern of the universe is an indisputable proof that all this has been made by One, and only One, Creator.'

When we see two identical watches, we need not be told that they are made in the same factory. On the same ground, when we see all the universe woven into a single entity; all its components being governed by the same laws, all its parts being operated on the same pattern, our instinct guides us to believe that it is created, made and controlled by ONE and ONLY ONE CREATOR.

Also, there is a great difference between the watches and the universe. Watches may be imitated or duplicated by imposters and forgers. But, as the scientists say, "by definition there is only one universe. One CANNOT repeat it or do experiments with it." So, we need not bother ourselves with the thought of any imitation-gods. If the universe - the thing MADE - cannot be more than one, HOW ALLAH - THE MAKER - can be more than ONE.

Now we should take a look at living things. There also we see the same uniformity of design in bone-structure. It is quite amusing to see the atheists use this uniformity to prove that there was no God. They say that "Because all the living beings are developed systematically and because, for instance, the skeletons of gibbon, orang-otan, chimpanzee, gorilla and man are quite similar in construction, it is proved that they have not been made by any Creator."

Suppose there had been no system in the universe nor in the structure of living beings and they had used that lack of method against the existence of any Creator, it could have made sense. But astonishingly enough, they are using the unique and perfect system of the universe and the living beings against the Omniscient and Omnipotent God. Any body can see the absurdity of this argument. Because the perfection of the universe is an irrefutable proof that it has not been made by a blind and senseless nature. Ironically, enough, they are using an argument which is basically against their claim.

Darwinists may use this single and uniform pattern of Creation against those who believe that different things were created by different gods. They may use it against those who say that, for instance, cow was created by a good-natured creator and the snake was made by an ill-natured god. But how can they use it against the belief in One Creator Who created all the things according to His own systematic plan.

It is quite obvious that Darwin failed in drawing the conclusion. He could not see the Eternal Truth which his evidence was pointing at. The evidence, gathered by him, is crying out loudly that all the universe, living or without life, has been created by ONE, and only ONE, ALLAH, Who is Omnipotent and Omniscient.

17. SEVEN REASONS WHY A SCIENTIST BELIEVES IN GOD

This article of Mr. A. Cressy Morrison, former president of the New York Academy of Sciences, first appeared in the *Reader's Digest* of January 1948; then on recommendation of Professor C.A. Coulson, F.R.S., professor of Mathematics at Oxford University, was republished in the *Reader's Digest* of November 1960. It shows how science compels the scientists to admit the essential need of a Supreme Creator.

"We are still in the dawn of the scientific age and every increase of light reveals more brightly the handiwork of an intelligent Creator. In the 90 years since Darwin we have made stupendous discoveries; with a spirit of scientific humility and of faith grounded in knowledge we are approaching even nearer to an awareness of God.

For myself, I count seven reasons for my faith.

First. By unwavering mathematical law we can prove that our universe was designed and executed by a great engineering Intelligence.

Suppose you put ten coins, marked from one to ten, into your pocket and give them a good shuffle. Now try to take them out in sequence from one to ten, putting back the coin each time and shaking them all again. Mathematically, we know that your chance of first drawing number one is one in ten; of drawing one and two in succession, one in 100; of drawing one, two and three in succession, one in a thousand, and so on. Your chance of drawing them all, from one to number ten in succession, would reach the unbelievable figure of one chance in ten thousand million.

By the same reasoning, so many exacting conditions are necessary for life on earth that they could not possibly exist in proper relationship by chance. The earth rotates on its axis at one thousand miles an hour; if it turned at one hundred miles an hour, our days and nights would be ten times as long as now, and the hot sun would then burn up our vegetation during each long day while in the long night any surviving sprout would freeze.

Again, the sun, source of our life, has a surface temperature of 12000 degree Fahrenheit, and our earth is just far enough away so that this "eternal fire" warms us just enough and not too much! If the sun gave off only one-half its present radiation, we would freeze, and if it gave half as much more, we would roast.

The slant of the earth, tilted at an angle of 23 degrees, gives us our seasons. If it had not been so tilted, vapors from the ocean would move north and south, piling up for us continents of ice. If our moon was, say, only 50,000 miles away instead of its actual distance, our tides would be so enormous that twice a day all continents would be submerged; even the mountains would soon be eroded away. If the crust of the earth had been only ten feet thicker, there would be no oxygen, without which animal life must die. Had the ocean been a few feet deeper, carbon dioxide and oxygen would have been absorbed and no vegetable life could exist. Or, if our atmosphere had been thinner, some of the meteors, now burned in space by the million every day, would be striking all parts of the earth, starting fires everywhere.

Because of these, and host of other examples, there is not one chance in million that life on our planet is an accident.

Second. The resourcefulness of life to accomplish its purpose is a manifestation of all-pervading Intelligence.

What life itself is no man has fathomed. It has neither weight nor dimensions, but it does have force; a growing root will crack a rock. Life has conquered water, land and air, mastering the elements, compelling them to dissolve and reform their combinations.

Life, the sculptor, shapes all living things; an artist, it designs every leaf of every tree and colors every flower. Life is a musician and has each bird to sing its love songs, the insects to call each other in the music of their multitudinous sounds. Life is a sublime chemist, giving taste to fruits and spices, and fragrance to the rose, changing water and carbonic acid into sugar and wood and, in so doing, releasing oxygen that animals may have the breath of life.

Behold an almost invisible drop of protoplasm, transparent and jelly-like, capable of motion, drawing energy from the sun. This single cell, this transparent mistlike droplet, holds within itself the germ of life, and has the power to distribute this life to every living thing, great and small. The powers of this droplet are greater than our vegetation and animals and people, for all life came from it. Nature did not create life; fire-blistered rocks and a saltless see could not meet the necessary requirements.

"Who, then, has put it here?"

Third. Animal wisdom speaks irresistibly of a good Creator who infused instinct into otherwise helpless little creatures.

The young salmon spends years at sea, then comes back to its own river, and travels up the very side of the river into which flows the tributary where it was born. What brings him back so precisely? If you transfer him to another tributary, he will know at once that he is off his course and he will fight his way down and back to the main stream and then turn up against the current to finish his destiny more accurately.

Even more difficult to solve is the mystery of eels. These amazing creatures migrate at maturity from all ponds and rivers everywhere - those from Europe across thousands of miles of ocean - all bound for the same abysmal deeps near Bermuda. There they breed and die. The little ones, with no apparent means of knowing anything except that they are in a wilderness of water, nevertheless find their way back not only to the very shore from which their parents came but thence to the rivers, lakes or little ponds - so that each body of water is always populated with eels. No American eels has ever been caught in Europe, no European eel in American waters. Nature has even delayed the maturity of the European eel by a year or more to make up for its longer journey. Where does the directing impulse originate?

A wasp will overpower a grasshopper, dig a hole in the earth, sting the grasshopper in exactly the right place so that he does not die but becomes unconscious and lives on as a form of preserved meat. Then the wasp will lay her eggs handily so that her children when they hatch, can nibble without killing the insect on which they feed: to them dead meat would be fatal. The mother then flies away and dies; she never sees her young. Surely, the wasp must have done all this right the first time and every time, or else there would be no wasp. Such mysterious techniques cannot be explained by adaptation; they were bestowed.

Fourth. Man has something more than animal instinct - the power of reason.

No other animal has ever left a record of its ability to count ten or even to understand the meaning of ten. Where instinct is like a single note of a flute, beautiful but limited, the human brain contains all the notes of all the instruments in the orchestra. No need to belabor this fourth point; thanks to the human reason we can contemplate the possibility that we are what we are only because we have received a spark of Universal Intelligence.

Fifth. Provision for all living is revealed in phenomena which we know today but which Darwin did not know - such as the wonder of genes. So unspeakably tiny are these genes that if all of them responsible for all living people in the world could be put in one place, there would be less than a thimbleful. Yet these ultramicroscopic genes and their companions, the chromosomes, inhabit every living cell and are the absolute keys to all human, animal and vegetable characteristics. A thimble is a small place in which to put all the individual characteristics of five thousand million human beings. However, the facts are beyond question. Well then, how do genes lock up all the normal heredity of a multitude of ancestors and preserve the psychology of each in such an infinitely small space? Here evolution really begins - at the cell, the entity which holds and carries genes. How a few million atoms, locked up as an ultramicroscopic gene, can absolutely rule all on earth is an example of profound cunning and provision that could emanate only from a Creative Intelligence - no other hypothesis will serve.

Sixth. By the economy of nature, we are forced to realize that only infinite wisdom could have foreseen and prepared with such astute husbandry.

Many years ago a species of cactus was planted in Australia as a protective fence. Having no insect enemies in Australia, the cactus soon began a prodigious growth; the alarming abundance persisted until the plants covered an area as long and wide as England, crowding inhabitants out of the towns and villages, and destroying their farms. Seeking a defence, the entomologists scoured the world; finally, they turned up an insect which exclusively feeds on cactus, and would eat nothing else. It would breed freely too; and it has no enemies in Australia. So animal soon conquered vegetable and today the cactus pest has retreated, and with it all but a small protective residue of the insects, enough to hold the cactus in check for ever.

Such checks and balances have been universally provided. We have not fast-breeding insects dominated the earth? Because they have no lungs such as man possesses; they breathe through tubes, But when insects grow large, their tubes do not grow in ratio to the increasing size of the body. Hence there has never been an insect of great size; this limitation has held them all in check.

If this physical check had not been provided, man could not exist. Imagine meeting a hornet as big as a lion!

Seventh. The fact that man can conceive the idea of God is in itself a unique proof.

The conception of god rises from a divine faculty of man, unshared with the rest of our world - the faculty we call imagination. By its power, man and man alone can find the evidence of things unseen. The vista that power opens up is unbounded; indeed, as man is perfected, imagination becomes a spiritual reality. He may discern in all the evidences of design and purpose the great truth that heaven is wherever and whatever is; that God is everywhere and in everything, but nowhere so close as in our hearts.

It is scientifically as well as imaginatively true; in the words of the Psalmist: The heavens declare the glory of God and the firmament sheweth His handiwork.

PART 2

18. MEANING OF "ONE"

Now that our talk is going to be centered on the theme "God is One," let us clarify what we mean by "One" in this sentence.

The word 'one' in our daily conversation conveys any of the following meanings:

(1) "Man" and "Horse" are one (because both are mammals). Here 'one' describes that both man and horse belong to the same genus (in Arabic jins).

(2) "Bakr" and "Smith" are one ... 'One' here shows that both are of the same species (in Arabic nau')

(3) You say pointing to two carpenters that they are one. Here 'one' means that both persons have same profession, or the same adjective can be used for both.

(4) Churchill was an orator, writer, soldier and statesman. You may say that his oratory, penmanship, soldiership and statesmanship were one, because they were combined in one person.

(5) One pint milk and one pint water are 'one,' because both have the same quantity.

(6) Hot milk and hot water are 'one,' because both are in the same condition.

(7) John and James are standing. You may say 'They are one,' because both are in the same position.

(8) George has two sons, William and Richard. William and Richard are one, because they have the same relation with George.

(9) A human body or a chair are one, because its components or parts are joined together. (But if the parts are taken apart or disintegrated, this 'one' will become millions).

(10) The beginning of counting is called 'one,' as the beginning theoretical line is called point. This 'one' is followed by countless numbers.

(11) A matchless or unique person or thing is called one, as, for example, we may say that the sun within our solar system is 'one' because it has no equal within this system.

BUT all these meanings of 'Unity' carry the idea of 'duality' or 'plurality,' because meanings No. 1 to 9 show that 'two' or 'more' things are 'one' in some respect. So, 'two' or 'more' are always present in these meanings.

'One' as beginning of number or count presupposes more than one thing.

A unique thing may be called one, but it is just a metaphorical use which has no relation with reality, because that unique thing, being made of matter, has millions of parts - is not one.

When we say 'God is One,' we take none of these meanings in consideration. Unity of God means that He has no parts, no body; He is not divisible even in imagination.

19. GOD CANNOT BE MORE THAN ONE

God cannot be more than one. Why this bold assertion? There are various reasons. In addition to some of the proofs given earlier, here are two proofs:

First Proof: It has been proved earlier that God is Eternal. And also it has been proved that Eternal cannot be a compound, mixture or mixed thing.

Now suppose there are two identical pens. They are similar in shape, size, color and all qualities. Still, they are two, each having a separate identity. So, each pen has two kinds of qualities: first, the common qualities which make one pen similar to the other; second, the distinguishing qualities which give each pen its separate entity and identity. In other words, each pen of the set is a compound of mixed lot of two separate properties.

This happens in all examples where two similar things exist side by side. It would surely happen if two Eternals were to exist side by side.

It means that if there were two Eternals they would both be compound. Each would have a common quality, i.e., Eternity; and a distinguishing quality which would give it a separate personality. This would mean that Eternal would be a compound, which we already have proved to be impossible.

Therefore, God being Eternal, cannot be more than one.

Second Proof: Suppose there were two gods. Could one of them over-ride the decision of the other one? If yes, then the second one is weaker than the first, and therefore is not omnipotent, not a god at all. If 'No,' then the first one is weaker than the second, and therefore not omnipotent, not a god at all.

And if both think and act exactly on similar lines, then what is the need to suppose two gods at all. One god is enough to run this universe!

20. MEANING OF 'SHIRK'

'Shirk' literally means 'partnership.' In Islamic terminology, it is used for the belief of 'polytheism' (believing in more than one god) and 'pantheism,' (believing that everything in the world is a part of god).

Polytheism is found in a variety of disguises. I propose to give this detail from the Urdu book <u>Unity and Justice of God</u> (Tauheed Aur 'Adl) of Maulana Muhammed Mustafa Jauhar of Karachi:

"Likewise, there is also difference of opinion about 'oneness' of God. For example:

"(1) Some say that God is not alone in Eternity. He has some colleague in His Eternity. As, for instance, Christians believe that Jesus Christ and Holy Ghost are partners of God in godhead - and it is evident that they could not be said to be partners in godhead unless they themselves were believed to be eternal.

"And the believers in transmigration of the soul believe that matter and soul both were eternal like God. If they discard the belief of the eternity of matter and soul, they will have to discard the belief of the transmigration of the soul also.

"(2) Resulting from the above belief, is the belief that there are partners in the virtues and qualities of God, as Christians believe about Jesus Christ. Because if Jesus Christ was not sharing the virtues and qualities of godhead, he could not be called a god.

"(3) Some groups believe that there were partners in the actions of God, i.e., they were His helpers or partners in creation and control of the universe, as the Greek philosophers believed in 'ten intellects' who created the whole universe.

"(4) Some people believe and say that God has no partner in His eternity, qualities and actions, but He has partners in worship.

Such people are mainly called 'Mushrik' in the Quranic terminology.

"Such Mushriks were the idol-worshippers of Arabia and their ideology is shared by the idol-worshippers in India and other places.

"(5) The last group is of those people who thought that God has no partner in His Eternity, virtues, actions and worship; but as He has given man wisdom and intellect, we have absolute right to decide what is good and what is evil in course of our actions. Thus they claimed to share with God the responsibility of legislating Sheriat. Such people were called 'Qadariyya' in Islam."

Thus we have five types of Shirk: (1) Shirk in the person and Eternity of God, (2) Shirk in the virtues of God, (3) Shirk in the Actions of God, (4) Shirk in the worship of God, and (5) Shirk in the Sheriat of God.

All such beliefs are vehemently and clearly rejected and refuted in the Quran.

21. THE HOLY PROPHET ON 'TAUHEEED'

I have already mentioned a discussion of the Holy Prophet with the atheists. It was a part of a great discussion in which 35 representatives of five religions (Jews, Christians, Atheists, Dualists i.e. the Parsees, and Polytheists i.e. the Mushrikeen) came to him and held discussion with him. In the end all accepted the truth of Islam and became Muslims.

The beauty of the arguments put by the Holy Prophet is in the fact that he explained highly philosophical subjects in such a simple language that even a layman could easily understand it. It is a masterpiece of "wisdom and good preaching."

By the way, there are people who assert day in and day out that the Holy Prophet learned from Judaism and Christianity. This discussion is a challenge to them. Let them produce such irrefutable argument from Jewish and Christian literature of early centuries before Islam.

It may be mentioned that these apparently simple aruguments hold their ground even today and they are as much valid today as they were 1400 years ago. The discussion is narrated by Imam Hasan Askari (a.s.) in his Tafseer and Allama Tabrasi has copied it in his famous 'Al-Ihtijaj (Vol. II). It has been translated, with short comments, into Urdu by Maulana Muhammed Mustafa Jauhar of Karachi and published twice. All three books are in my library.

The Holy Prophet had started his talks with Jews, then went on conversing with Christians, atheists, dualists and lastly with the idol-worshippers.

The arrangement of my booklet has compelled me to give the arguments against atheists in the first part. Now I am giving here the remaining four discussions.

22. ISLAM VERSUS JUDAISM

Jews of Arabia in the days of Holy Prophet had lost their original beliefs. Being in touch with the Christians and the idol-worshippers, they also had started the dogma of God having a son. As Uzair ('Esdras' in English) had re-written Torah, after it had been lost for centuries, Jews revered him very much and started the claim that Uzair was the Son of God.

The Holy Prophet asked them what was the reason of their belief. They said that Uzair re-wrote Torah for the children of Israel when it was lost to them and it shows that he was the son of God.

The Holy Prophet: Why Uzair was son of God and Moses was not, as Moses brought Torah from God for the first time and bringing it first time is far more important than re-writing it?

Moreover, Moses showed many miracles which Uzair did not show. Therefore, if Uzair was son of God because God gave him the honor of re-writing Torah, Moses is far more deserving to be the son of God.

Also, I take it that by sonship you do not mean that relationship which is established when a child is born from the womb of his mother after his parents establish sexual intercourse. Jews confirmed it saying that when they said that Uzair was son of God, they did not mean sonship by birth, but because of his honor with God. It has the same meaning as many teachers call their favorite pupil "my son."

The Holy Prophet said that he already had answered that argument when he said that by that standard Moses was more deserving to be called "Son of God."

And so far as the example of an elder calling some unrelated youth as "my son" is concerned, let us look at such uses a bit further.

You must have seen that the same elder, while showing respect to some great scholar, calls him "my brother" or "my elder" or "my chief" or even "my father."

Basing on such usage, will you say that Moses (who was more honored than Uzair before God) should be called "Brother of God" or "Elder of God" or "Chief of God?"

The Jews could not answer this argument and after some deliberation accepted Islam.

23. UNITY VERSUS TRINITY

Christians had expressed their belief that God is one with Jesus and that Jesus was son of God.

The Holy Prophet asked them what they meant by saying that Eternal God is one with his son Jesus?

Do you mean that the Eternal (i.e. God) became mortal as Jesus was?

If you say so, it is impossible that eternal which has neither beginning or end should become mortal, which has both beginning and end. Or do you mean that mortal (Jesus) became eternal as God is?

But this also is impossible, because how can a thing which was created after non-existence be eternal?

Or do you mean by this sentence (God is one with Jesus) that God gave Jesus honor which was not given to anyone?

If so, then you will have to accept that Jesus was not eternal, as he was created; and that his quality of getting honor from God is also not eternal, because he got it after his being created. And in that case, Jesus cannot be one with God because eternal and transient cannot combine together.

Christians: When God showed many wonderful miracles on the hand of Jesus, He made him His son as an honor.

Holy Prophet: You just heard what I told the Jews (on the subject of Uzair and sonship of God). And repeated the previous argument. The Christians could not answer the arguments.

Then after some deliberation one of them said that the scriptures have reported Jesus as saying, "I am going to my father." (This argument is based on the understanding that Jesus himself claimed that God was his father, and as the Holy Prophet accepted Jesus as a true prophet, his claim could not be wrong).

The Holy Prophet said that the wording is "I am going to my and your father." It means that all persons in the whole audience were sons of God in the same sense in which Jesus was son of God.

Further, this quotation refutes your claim that Jesus was son of God because of the unique honor he had before God, because, according to your own belief, none among the audience had that honor and still they were called to be sons of God.

After some deliberation they became Muslims.

24. UNITY VERSUS DUALITY

Dualists (present day Parsees) believe that Light and Darkness are Creator and Ruler of the universe. The Holy Prophet asked them the reason for this belief.

They said: We find two kinds of things in this world - good and evil. These are opposites and we believe that the creator of good cannot be the creator of evil, and vice verse. These two opposites cannot be found together.

Do you not see that snow cannot give warmth and fire cannot make cool? That is why we believe two separate creators for good and evil and they are represented by Light and Darkness and both are eternal.

The Holy Prophet said: Pray tell me, have you not found in this world different colors - black, white, red, yellow, green and blue? Is it not a fact that none of these colors can be found with another color in the same place at the same time?

Dualists: Yes. No two of these colors can be found in one place at the same time.

The Holy Prophet said: Then, according to your thinking, you must believe that there is a separate creator for each of these colors.

The Dualists could not give any answer to that argument.

Then the Holy Prophet asked them that Light and Darkness being opposites, how did it happen that both have joined hands in creation and their creatures (good and evil) are together in this world? Doesn't it mean that there is a superior power who has brought these opposites together?

They took time pondering upon these points and finally accepted Islam.

25. UNITY VERSUS IDOL-WORSHIP

Then the Holy Prophet asked the idol-worshippers why they worshiped the idols instead of the One Almighty God?

They said: We seek to be nearer to God through these idols.

Holy Prophet: Do these idols hear? Are they pious and obedient servants of God? How can you seek nearness to God through them?

Idol-worshippers: No. They do not hear.

Holy Prophet: And the fact is that you have carved these idols by your own hands. So, if these had ability to worship, it was incumbent upon them to worship you (because you are their creator) not that you should worship them.

Moreover, God has never allowed you to worship the idols (so how can you be nearer to God through these idols, without any authority from God?)

On hearing this argument, the idol-worshippers split into three groups.

One group said: These are the images of those persons in whom God was incarnated. Thus we worship God by worshipping the images of those persons who were incarnations of God.

The Holy Prophet said:

1. Your belief that God was incarnated in any body is absolutely wrong because you have made the Creator like His creatures. Don't you see that God cannot be incarnated in anything unless that thing surrounds God? (But how can anything surround God?).

2. Also what will be the difference between God and other things which are found in a body (like color, taste, smell, hardness or softness, heaviness or lightness)? All these things are found in other things, and have no independent existence. Is God also like this?

3. Lastly, when you attribute to God a quality (incarnation) which is the quality of a transient (of a thing which was created after non-existence), then why not believe that all qualities of a transient are found in Him? I mean that you must also believe that God changes and deteriorates and dies, because the body of His supposed incarnation changes and deteriorates and dies. It is impossible for the content not to change with the changes of the receptacle!

All these considerations prove that it is impossible for God to be incarnated in anybody.

And when incarnation is wrong, there remains no basis for your belief that God incarnated in some of his creatures and that these idols are the images of such persons.

The second group said that those idols were the images of those past generations who were very obedient to God. "We carved their images and worship them with a view to glorify God through their worship."

The Holy Prophet asked them: Pray tell me what kind of worship have you saved for Almighty God, when you are worshipping these images by prostrating before them, praying to them, and putting your head before them?

Don't you know that it is the right of God that He should not be thought equal to His servant? If you honor a King in the same way as you honor His servant, will it not be an insult to the King?

The Holy Prophet then added: Don't you realize that by worshipping the images of the creatures, you are insulting the Creator?

The idol-worshippers agreed that it is so.

The last group said: "God created Adam and ordered the angels to prostrate before him. We deserve more to prostrate before Adam (because we are his children). As Adam is not alive today, we have carved his image to prostrate before it and to seek nearness to God through that worship."

The Holy Prophet told them: Agreed that God ordered the angels to prostrate before Adam. But, has He ordered you to prostrate before the image of Adam? Adam and his image are not one and the same thing. How are you sure that God is not displeased with your prostration before Adam's image?

Look at it in this way. If a man allows you to enter his house one day, do you have any right to enter that house next day? Or to enter his house the same day?

If a man gives you a gift of one of his clothes, or one of his horses, are you justified in taking it?

Idol-worshippers: Yes, we will take it.

The Holy Prophet: If you don't accept that cloth or horse, do you have any right to take his other clothes or horses without his permission?

Idol-worshippers: No. Because he had given the first cloth or the horse as a gift but not the other.

The Holy Prophet: Who has more right that his property should not be used without his permission: God or His creatures?

Idol-worshippers: God has more right that His property should not be infringed upon.

The Holy Prophet: Then why are you contravening this principle? When and where has God allowed you to worship the idols?

After some consideration, all of them became Muslims.

PART 3

26. TAUHEED OF ISLAM

It will be seen from the above-mentioned discussion how Islam, for the first time in the history of religions, explained <u>Tauheed</u> (Oneness of God) in such a way that there was no misunderstanding afterwards.

Though the Jews believed in One God, theirs was not the universal but tribal god. And even then, they had fallen into the pitfall of giving Uzair the title of 'son of God.'

It is the direct result of the teaching of Islam that Jews left calling a man 'son of God.' Christians are trying to re-interpret the dogma of Trinity; Hindus were compelled to rediscover that Vedas teach Unity of God and that idol-worship was wrong.

The Sura of Tauheed is one of the shortest suras of Quran. It establishes the pure belief in the oneness of God, rejecting all types of 'shirk' in these words:

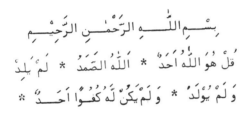

In the Name of Allah, the Beneficent, the Merciful

"Say: He is God, the One and Only; God, the Eternal, the Absolute;
He begetteth not, nor is He begotten;
And there is none like unto Him."   **(Sura 112)**

The first sentence of the Islamic Creed, i.e., "There is no god except Allah," leads a Muslim throughout his life not only in religious matters but in social behavior also. "There is no god" shows a Muslim that nothing in the universe is superior to him. It is observed in Quran that "Allah has created everything for your benefit." So a Muslim knows that nothing in this world is to be worshipped. Neither stone nor trees, neither animals nor human beings; neither the sun, nor the moon, nor the stars can be worshipped, because everything is created, and created for his benefit. When a Muslim thus has rejected every falsehood and every idea of nature-worship, idol-worship or human worship, he is ready to believe in the positive truth of the Unity of God.

Believing in a Supreme Being gives an aim to our life and provides a purpose for our actions. Had a man been left with the wrong impression that there was no God at all, his life would have been aimless, and an aimless life is dangerous. So it is added that there is no god "except Allah." This sentence has a negative as well as a positive aspect. Both are instrumental in creating the belief that every man is equal to every other person. When nobody is superior, nobody is inferior. Thus, the belief in the Unity of God promotes the sense of brotherhood and equality and equity which is another feature of Islam.

27. ATTRIBUTES OF GOD

Now time has come to explain briefly what is our belief concerning God. In preceding chapters I have discussed almost all the aspects of our belief. It should be apparent by now that there are many attributes which are a MUST for God, while there are others which are beneath His dignity and cannot be found in Him.

Therefore, in our faith, the attributes of Allah have been grouped as 'positive' and 'negative.'

SIFAT-E-THUBUTIYYAH

The positive attributes which are befitting Allah are called Sifat-e-Thubutiyyah. They are many in number, but only eight of them are usually mentioned. They are:

1. QADEEM: It means that Allah is Eternal, i.e., He has neither beginning nor end. Nothing except Allah is eternal.

2. QAADIR: It means that Allah is Omnipotent, i.e., He has power over every thing and every affair.

3. AALIM: It means that Allah is Omniscient, i.e., He knows every thing. Even our unspoken intentions and desires are not hidden from Him.

4. HAI: It means that Allah was always alive and will remain alive for ever.

5. MUREED: It means that Allah has His own Will and discretion in all affairs. He does not do anything under compulsion.

6. MUDRIK: It means that He is All-Perceiving, as 'Sami' (All-Hearing), 'Baseer' (All-Seeing), 'Hadhir' (Omnipresent). Allah sees and hears every thing without any need of eyes or ears.

7. MUTAKALLIM: It means that Allah is the Master of the Word, i.e., He can create speech in anything as He did in a tree for Hadhret Musa (a.s.), and in the 'Curtain of Light' for our Holy Prophet (s.a.w.).

8. SADIQ: It means that Allah is true in His words and promises. It is impossible to fix any limit to His attributes. This list is not exhaustive but is essential to understand the Glory of Allah.

The attibutes are not acquired but are inherent in the conception of Divinity.

SIFAT-E-SALBIYYAH

The Negative Attributes which cannot be found in Allah because they are below His dignity, are called Sifat-e-Salbiyyah. They are many, but like Sifat-e-Thubutiyyah, only eight are listed here. They are:

1. **SHAREEK:** The word "Shareek" means a colleague or partner. Allah has neither a colleague nor a partner in His Divinity.

2. **MURRAKKAB**: This word means "compound" or "mixed." Allah is neither made, nor composed, of any material. He cannot be divided even in the imagination.

3. **MAKAAN:** It means "place." Allah is not in a place because He has no JISM (body), and He is everywhere because His power and knowledge is magnificently apparent everywhere.

4. **HULOOL:** It means "entering." Nothing enters into Allah nor does He enter into anything or anybody. Therefore, the belief of Incarnation in any form is abhorrent to the conception of Divinity.

5. **MAHALLE HAWADITH:** This means "subject to changes." Allah cannot change.

6. **MAR-I:** It means "visible." Allah is not visible. He has not been seen, is not seen and will never be seen.

7. **IHTIYAJ:** It means "dependence" or "need." Allah is not deficient in any virtue, so He does not need anything. He is All-Perfect.

8. **SIFAT-E-ZA-ID:** This means "added qualifications." The attributes of Allah are not separate from His Being. When we say that God is Omnipotent and Merciful, we do not mean that His Power and Mercy are something different from His Person. We see that a child is born without any power, and then he acquires strength day by day. It is so because power is not his person. But God is not like this. He is Power Himself; Knowledge Himself; Justice Himself; Virtue Himself; Truth Himself, and so on.

It will thus be seen that according to Islam, ALLAH is the name of God as perceived in the light of the above Positive and Negative Attributes. In other words, ALLAH is the Creator of the Universe, Self-Existent, the Source of all Perfection, and free from all defects.

28. NAMES OF ALLAH

The proper name which Islam uses for God is "ALLAH." ALLAH means "One Who deserves to be loved" and "into Whom everyone seeks refuge."

This word, grammatically speaking, is unique. It has no plural and no feminine. So this name itself reflects light upon the fact that Allah is One and Only One; He has neither any partner nor any equal. The name cannot properly be translated by the word "God" because God can be transformed into "Gods" and "Goddesses."

Two more frequently used names are Rahman and Rahim.

Rahman signifies that Allah is Merciful and that His Mercy encompasses each and everything in the universe without any distinction on account of faith or belief. He makes, creates and sustains everything and every man whether he be a Muslim or kafir.

Rahim signifies that the Mercy of Allah on the Day of Judgment will surround the true believers only, and that unbelievers and hypocrites will be left out.

It is apparent that both of these names signify a distinct aspect of God's Mercy. His Mercy in this world, as signified by "Rahman" is general; and the one in the life-hereafter, as signified by "Rahim" is special.

It will be of interest to note that the word "Rahman" cannot be used except for Allah, while "Rahim" can be used for others also.

That is why it has been told by Imam that "Rahman is a reserved name which denotes unreserved Mercy" and "Rahim is an unreserved name which denotes Reserved Mercy."

29. AL-ASMA-UL-HUSNA

Here is a list of 99 names for Allah in Islam, together with their meanings:

No.	Name of Allah		Meaning
1.	الله _	*Allāh*	Proper Name of the One and Only God.
2.	الرّحمن	*ar-Raḥmān*	The Merciful.
3.	الرّحيم	*ar-Raḥim*	The Compassionate.
4.	الملك	*al-Malik*	The Ruler.
5.	القدّوس	*al-Quddūs*	The Holy.
6.	السّلام	*as-Salām*	The Safety.
7.	المؤمن	*al-Mu'min*	The Trusted.
8.	المهيمن	*al-Muhaymin*	The Protector.
9.	العزيز	*al-'Aziz*	The Powerful.
10.	الجبّار	*al-Jabbār*	The Most Powerful.
11.	المتكبّر	*al-Mutakabbir*	The Magnificent.
12.	الخالق	*al-Khālik*	The Creator.

13.	الباري	*al-Bāri*	The Creator (from nothing).
14.	المصوّر	*al-Muṣawwir*	The Designer.
15.	الغفّار	*al-Ghaffār*	The Forgiver.
16.	القهّار	*al-Qahhār*	The Almighty, The Subduer.
17.	الوهّاب	*al-Wahhāb*	The Giver.
18.	الرزّاق	*ar-Razzāq*	The Provider; The Sustainer.
19.	الفتّاح	*al-Fattāḥ*	The Opener.
20.	العليم	*al-'Alīm*	The Omniscient; The All-Knowing.
21.	القابض	*al-Qābiḍ*	The Gatherer.
22.	الباسط	*al-Bāsiṭ*	The Expander.
23.	الخافض	*al-Khāfiḍ*	The Humbler.
24.	الرّافع	*ar-Rāfi'*	The Raiser.
25.	المذلّ	*al-Mudhill*	The Subduer.
26.	المعزّ	*al-Mu'izz*	The Exalter.
27.	السّميع	*as-Samī'*	The All-Hearing.
28.	البصير	*al-Baṣīr*	The All-Seeing.
29.	الحكم	*al-Ḥakam*	The Arbitrator.
30.	العدل	*al-'Adl*	The Justice; The Just.
31.	اللّطيف	*al-Laṭīf*	The Kind.
32.	الخبير	*al-Khabīr*	The All-Knowing.
33.	الحليم	*al-Ḥalīm*	The Clement.
34.	العظيم	*al-'Aẓīm*	The Great.
35.	الغفور	*al-Ghafūr*	The Forgiver.
36.	الشّكور	*ash-Shakūr*	The Thankful.
37.	العليّ ـ	*al-'Ali*	The High.
38.	الكبير	*al-Kabīr*	The Great.

39.	الحفيظ	*al-Ḥafiẓ*	The Protector.
40.	المقيت	*al-Muqīt*	The Nourisher.
41.	الحسيب	*al-Ḥasīb*	The Reckoner.
42.	الجليل	*al-Jalīl*	The Honorable.
43.	الكريم	*al-Karīm*	The Generous.
44.	الرّقيب	*ar-Raqīb*	The Guard.
45.	المجيب	*al-Mujīb*	The One Who answers (the prayers).
46.	الواسع	*al-Wāsiʿ*	The Enricher.
47.	الحكيم	*al-Ḥakīm*	The Wise.
48.	الودود	*al-Wadūd*	The Affectionate.
49.	المجيد	*al-Majīd*	The Glorious.
50.	الماجد	*al-Mājid*	The Honorable.
51.	الباعث	*al-Bāʿith*	The Resurrector.
52.	الشّهيد	*ash-Shahīd*	The Witness.
53.	الحقّ	*al-Ḥaqq*	The Truth.
54.	الوكيل	*al-Wakīl*	The Trustee.
55.	القوى	*al-Qawī*	The Powerful.
56.	المتين	*al-Matīn*	The Strong.
57.	الولى	*al-Walī*	The Guardian.
58.	الحميد	*al-Ḥamīd*	The Praiseworthy.
59.	المحصى	*al-Muḥṣi*	The Reckoner.
60.	المبدىء	*al-Mubdi*	The Beginner; The Creator.
61.	المعيد	*al-Muʿīd*	The Returner; The Resurrector.
62.	المحيى	*al-Muḥyi*	The Bestower of Life.
63.	المميت	*al-Mumīt*	The Bringer of Death.
64.	الحىّ	*al-Ḥayy*	The Living.

65.	القيّوم	al-Qayyūm	The Self-existing.
66.	الواحد	al-Wāḥid	The One.
67.	الاحد	al-Aḥad	The Only; The Unique.
68.	الصّمد	aṣ-Ṣamad	The Perfect; The Eternal.
69.	القادر	al-Qādir	The Omnipotent.
70.	المقتدر	al-Muqtadir	The All-powerful.
71.	المقدّم	al-Muqaddim	The Advancer.
72.	المؤخّر	al-Mu'akkhir	The Keeper behind.
73.	الأوّل	al-Awwal	The First.
74.	الاخر	al-Ākhir	The Last.
75	الظّاهر	aẓ-Ẓāhir	The Apparent.
76.	الباطن	al-Bāṭin	The Hidden.
77.	المولى	al-Mawlā	The Master.
78.	المتعالى	al-Muta'ālī	The Most High.
79.	البارّ	al-Bārr	The Beneficent.
80.	التّوّاب	at-Tawwāb	The Forgiver.
81.	المنتقم	al-Muntaqim	The Avenger.
82.	العفوّ	al-'Afuww	The Forgiver.
83.	الرّوءف	ar-Ra'ūf	The Compassionate.
84.	مالك الملك	Māliku 'l-Mulk	The Sovereign of the Kingdom (Universe).
85.	ذوالجلال والاكرام	Dhu 'l-Jalāl wa 'l-Ikrām	The Owner of Glory and Honor.
86.	المقسط	al-Muqsiṭ	The Just.
87.	الجامع	al-Jāmi'	The One Who brings together; The Comprehensive.
88.	الغنىّ	al-Ghaniyy	The Rich; The Self-Sufficient.

89.	المغنى	al-Mughnī	The Bestower of Richness.
90.	المانع	al-Māni'	The Prohibiter.
91.	الضّارّ	aḍ-Ḍārr	The Bringer of Adversity.
92.	النّافع	an-Nāfi'	The Beneficial.
93.	النّور	an-Nūr	The Light.
94.	الهادى	al-Hādī	The Guide.
95.	البديع	al-Badi'	The Maker (with previous example).
96.	الباقى	al-Bāqī	The Everlasting.
97.	الوارث	al-Wārith	The Inheriter.
98.	الرّشيد	ar-Rashīd	The Guide.
99.	الصّبور	aṣ-Ṣabūr	The Patient.

30. ATTRIBUTES OF PERSON AND ACTION

Question: One of the names of Allah is 'Khaalique' i.e., Creator. As Allah was Creator from ever, does it not follow that the created things, i.e., the universe is from ever?

Answer: Allah was not creating from ever. If you study properly, you will find that the attributes of God, as mentioned in the last chapter of the booklet, *God of Islam,* may easily be divided into two groups.

First, there are those attributes which can never be separated from the conception of Divinity. For example, we say that God is Qaadir (Omnipotent); Aalim (Omniscient); and Hai (Everliving). These are such attributes which can never be separated from the conception of God, because there never was a time when God was not Omnipotent, Omniscient or Living. He was Qaadir, Aalim and Hai for ever, and will remain Qaadir, Aalim, and Hai for ever.

Such attributes refer to the person of Allah, and are, therefore, called <u>Sifat-e-Dhat</u> (Attributes of Person of God).

Second, there are the attributes which describe the actions of Allah. For example, we say that Allah is 'Khaalique' (Creator),

'Razique' (Sustainer) etc. These are the Attributes which describe the actions of Allah, and are, therefore, called Sifat-e-Af'aal (Attributes of Actions of Allah).

These actions were not from ever, and therefore, these attributes were not used for Allah from ever. You know that Allah is 'Mureed.' He acts according to His own plan and His Own Will. He is not like fire which burns without any intention or will of its own. Nor is He like the sun which goes on giving light and heat without intention and will of its own. Allah works according to His Own plan. He created when He wanted, and not before that.

It does not mean that God has no power to create. The power to create was there for ever; because the 'Power' is not separate from His person. But the appearance of that power, and bringing it into effect, was not from ever. In short, Allah had power to create from ever, but He did not create from ever. And when He created, He was called Khaalique; but not before that.

Likewise, when God sustained, He was called 'Razique'; when He forgave, He was called 'Ghaffar'; when He avenged, He was called 'Qahhaar'; when He gave life, He was called 'Muhyi'; and when He gave death, He was called 'Mumeet.'